To DEAREST YVONNE –

WITH OUR LOVE FOR A VERY HAPPY CHRISTMAS!
HOPE THIS WILL BRING MANY SOUTH AFRICAN
SIGHTS AND MEMORIES TO MIND.
GOD BLESS YOU –

Mom, Dad, Brendon, Daël & NATALIE

9.1

WITH OUR LOVE FOR A VERY HAPPY CHRISTMAS!
HOPE THIS WILL BRING MANY SOUTH AFRICAN
SIGHTS AND MEMORIES TO MIND.
GOD BLESS YOU –

Mom, Dad, Brendon, Daël & NATALIE

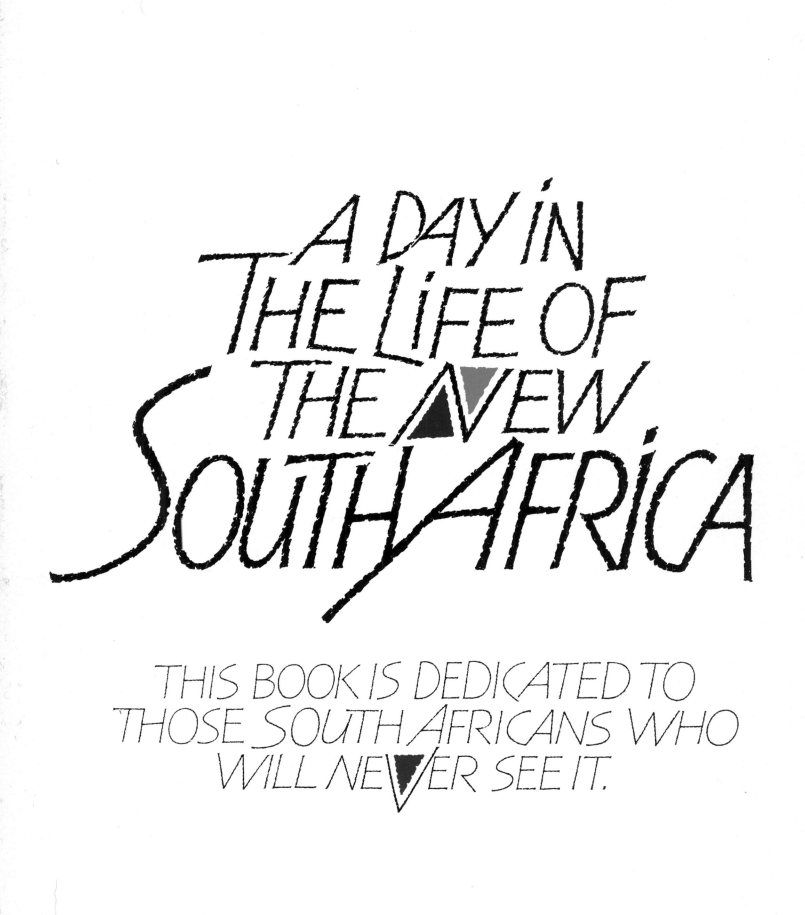

A DAY IN THE LIFE OF THE NEW SOUTH AFRICA

THIS BOOK IS DEDICATED TO
THOSE SOUTH AFRICANS WHO
WILL NEVER SEE IT.

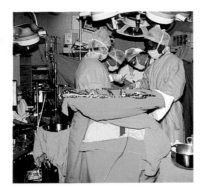

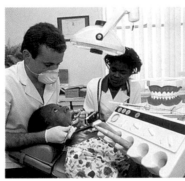

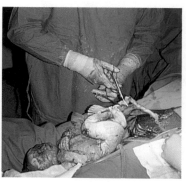

"A Day in the Life of the New South Africa" is printed on 135 gsm Shaka Gloss manufactured by **Sappi Fine Papers.**

Published by **The South African National Council for the Blind** with eager and expert assistance from Colin Hall, Bob Thornley and Di Pieterse.

Copy written by **Dr William Rowland, Vanessa Bouwer and Janessa Urquhart.**

Designed by **Peter Stuckey and Wendy Matthews of Photo-prints, Cape Town.**

Cover design by **Abdul Amien.**

Reproduction by **Photo-prints (Pty) Ltd, Cape Town.**

Printed and bound by **CTP Book Printers, Cape Town.**

ISBN 0-9583840-1-0

MESSAGE FROM
PRESIDENT NELSON MANDELA

The first edition of this book in 1982 was a remarkable achievement – a day in the life of ordinary South Africans captured on camera by fellow South Africans. The photographs certainly reflected the life and times of our country and its people during that troubled period of our history.

Following the tremendous success of the 1982 edition, it is fitting that the second edition was photographed three months after the first democratic election in our country, using the same winning formula. I feel this 1994 edition is a manifestation of the new spirit which is sweeping our nation. The photographs themselves speak more eloquently about the hopes and dreams of our fellow South Africans during this period of reconstruction than words ever could.

This book is the result of the enthusiasm of thousands of professional and amateur photographers, the generosity of sponsors, the contributions of numerous private individuals, and the commitment of a willing team dedicated to a worthy cause. In so many ways, this epitomises the spirit of the New South

PHOTOGRAPH: KARINA TUROK

Africa. Achievements such as this surely prove that South Africans have the will and determination to ensure the success of reconciliation and nation-building.

I would like to congratulate the South African National Council for the Blind on this unique fund-raising project. The people they are dedicated to serve will not be able to appreciate the final product of their efforts, but will benefit from the proceeds of the sale of this book.

Finally, I wish to thank each and every person who participated and contributed towards this historical book, and wish this project the success it so richly deserves. I hope we do not have to wait another twelve years for the third edition, which will surely reflect the realisation of many of the hopes and dreams of our multi-cultural society.

Mandela

The promotion of the third day of August, 1994, and the realisation of this book, would not have been possible without the material support of our core sponsors.

To these generous partners, we extend our grateful thanks.

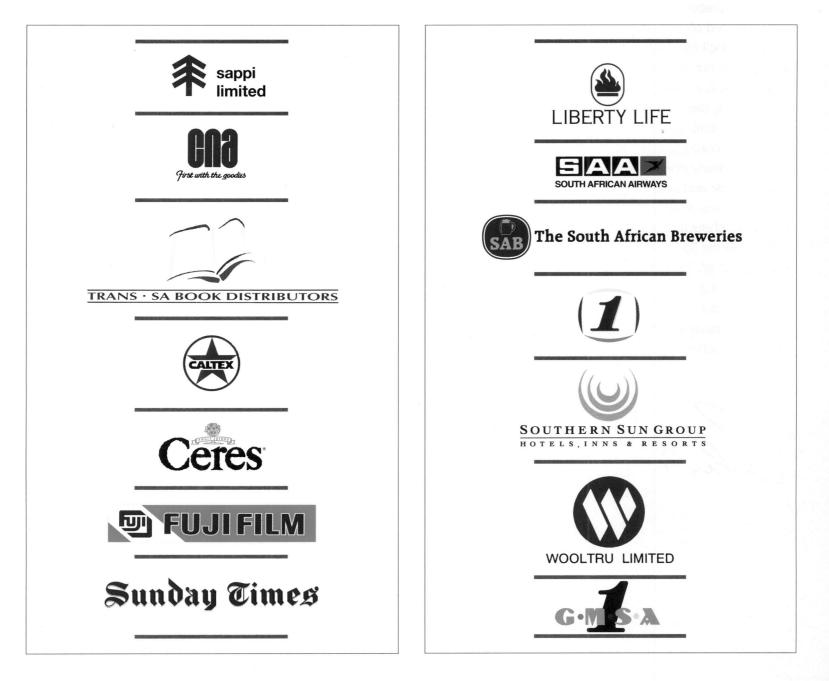

FROM COLIN HALL
PROJECT PATRON

Some 12 years ago, I led a project known as "A Day in the Life of South Africa". On a chosen day, all South Africans were invited to take photographs and to submit them for judging. The photographic record was published in the form of a book which has become truly Africana. The project operated on the basis that the only group to benefit financially would be blind people so all profits were donated to the South African National Council for the Blind to build a rehabilitation centre for newly blinded people.

I was greatly honoured to have been approached by the South African National Council for the Blind to be the Patron of "A Day in the Life of the **New** South Africa". Like the first, it was a truly remarkable project which was initiated at a vital time in the history of our country. In a sense it heralds the new beginning of our rekindled nation.

What started off as a fund-raising project of the South African National Council for the Blind culminated in an event that united the people of our country on one single day – 3 August 1994.

This book is a manifestation of our country – its aspirations and aversions, dreams and dilemmas. It is an expression of the hope and optimism the people of South Africa have for our magnificent country and its people.

What is clearly evident from the photographs is a renewed sense of pride and patriotism. I was overwhelmed by the hope and promise for our country that was realised through this national event. The remarkable spirit which was prominently characteristic of the polling queues was once again explicitly apparent.

This book the South African National Council for the Blind have presented to us serves as an historic gift to all South Africans. I would like to thank the project team for their commitment, the dedication of many, many hours and their never ending enthusiasm.

Our beautiful country has been exposed, our dreams have been divulged and our people have been revealed. May you treasure this book and the hope and potential for our country it reflects.

FROM WILLIAM ROWLAND
EXECUTIVE DIRECTOR
SOUTH AFRICAN NATIONAL COUNCIL FOR THE BLIND

W hat is it that people looked forward to through the long bitter years of political conflict? – Freedom? Peace? A new beginning? A better life?

And what do these things actually mean now that the time of change has come?

Perhaps we can discover the answer simply by observing ordinary South Africans as they go about their everyday lives. On 3 August 1994, as people took pictures of other people, of things and events all over the country, they were – without knowing it – creating for posterity an historical record of what it really was like to be a citizen of the New South Africa at the very start.

There are the moments of joy in the birth of a baby and the reunion of loved ones. There is the experience of deep sorrow around an open grave. But for most 3 August was no more than a routine day of normal activities – riding in taxis, catching fish, joking with friends, playing pool. We see the street children and the hoboes, the drug pushers and the priests, the workers and the politicians; we see a land of the starkest contrasts, misery and beauty, squatter shacks and luxurious dwellings, where poor people hunt for food while others take their pick from the horn of plenty.

This is the very stuff of life, all over the world and also in our own country. But how is it different? Is life in the New South Africa nothing more than is depicted in these multiple images?

Assuredly, it is much, much more, because the experiences and events here recorded are taking place in a country transformed. What we discover in these remarkable pages is "a rainbow nation" in a country of reborn hope. Each of the 16 138 photographs we received tells an individual story, but all of the pictures together also tell a collective story, of optimism and patriotism, of pride in being South African. The spirit of renewal – according to the judging panel – was irrepressibly present throughout.

In 1982, when we staged the first "A Day in the Life" project I realized that the event would one day be repeatable in a post-apartheid South Africa. But I also believed that the day would be a long time in the coming – two or three decades at least. The fact that only twelve years later we have been able to restage the event is, it seems to me, truly a miracle. This book celebrates that miracle.

00h00
06h00

The early hours of the morning know no distinction between the waking hours for some South Africans and the working hours of others. The fading shadow of the moon collectively captures serene sleeping moments and arduous hours of labour. The transcendence from darkness into light intensifies the contrast and diversity of our country and its people.

The joys of youth are celebrated in the early hours of a new day. And the birth of a baby heralds the gift of life. But the desperation of others intensifies as the darkness surrenders to the break of a new day which in the past has held no promise of hope. But it is a new day in the New South Africa where the window of opportunity has been opened to liberate our patient people and unleash their concealed potential.

1, C. SCHOEMAN

2. M. GUINAN-BROWN

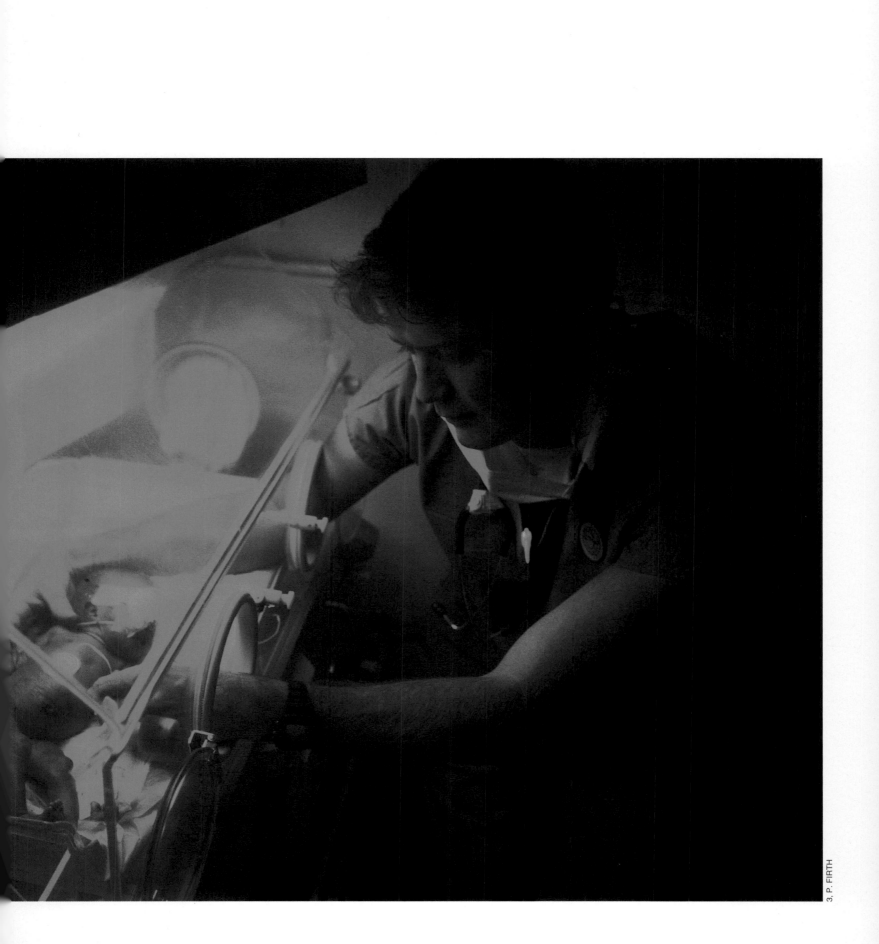

3. P. FIRTH

4. D. VAN DER MERWE

5. D. VAN DER MERWE

6. J. VAN TONDER

7. L. L. LE GRANGE

9. R. WILSON

12. C. VILJOEN

13. C. SCHOEMAN

14, R. WILSON

15, M. NAPIER

16, A. WELZ

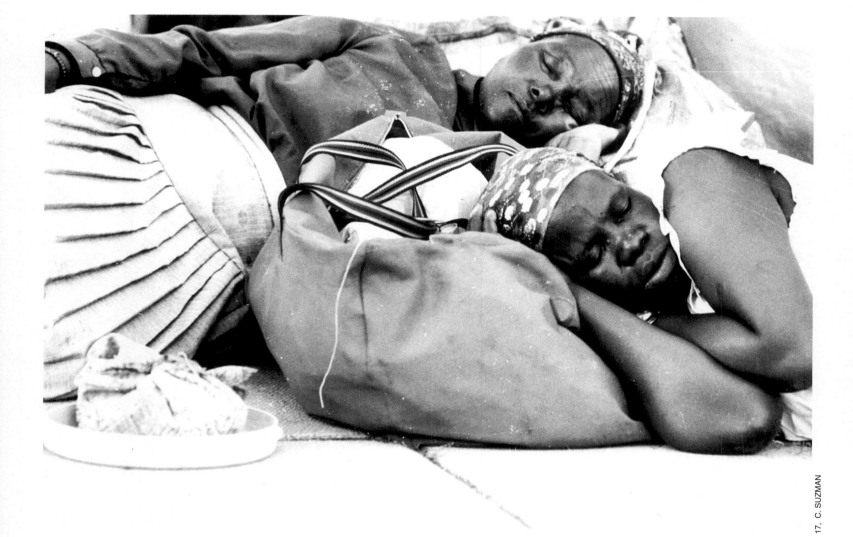

17, C. SUZMAN

19, E. B. L. LIGHTBODY

OPPOSITE PAGE
18, B. DU TOIT

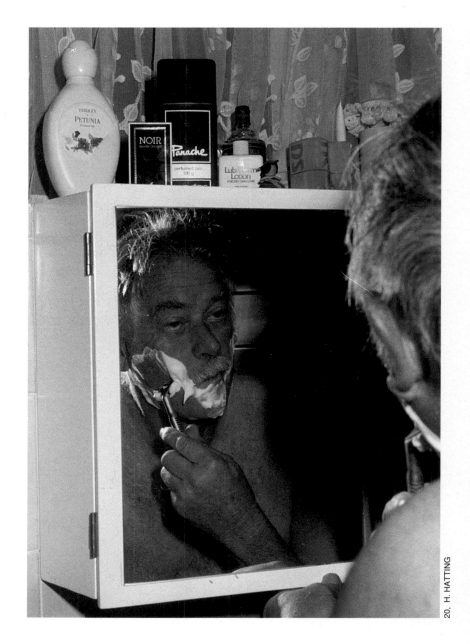

20, H. HATTING

06h00
09h00

Morning has broken. South Africa awakes. As a new day unfolds people and animals begin to surface and the story of their lives is exposed through the camera's lens. The pace begins to hasten as our land in the sun warms to the first gentle rays of light.

The feeling of harmony and solidarity is condensed in the routine of our daily lives. School children dawdle as businessmen dash to meet early morning deadlines. Some face the day with the joy of new life as others are faced with the sorrow of burying a loved one. And photographers look on to capture the joy and sorrow of these passing moments to make them eternal.

22, N. KLOPPERS

23, D. DALLAS

24, I. MULLER

25, A. PIKE

26, P. HEADLEY

27, S. M. HARDY

28. H. FRANKENFELD

29. R. PIENAAR

30. J. HRUSA

31. J. HRUSA

OPPOSITE PAGE
32, D. SAUNDERS

33. R. MATTHEWS

34, R. ELLIOT

35, D. WEST

36, H. ORBAN

OPPOSITE PAGE
37, R. MATTHEWS

38, H. FRANKENFELD

39, H. FRANKENFELD

40. S. STAUB

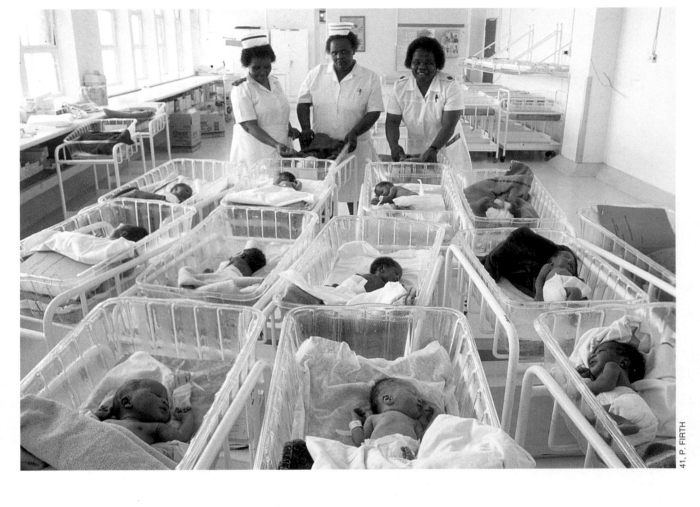

41, P. FIRTH

42, H. BRINK

44, P. SCHEDLER

45, C. K. MUIR

VOTE FOR JOBS, PEACE AND FREEDOM.

ANC

46. A. OLWAGEN

47. P. HEADLEY

48. R. MATTHEWS

49, J. MCKINNELL

OPPOSITE PAGE
50, R. FORD

51, I. MULLER

54. J. BAPTISE

55. J. MCGREGOR

56. S. KRUGER

57, D. ROUX

58, P. R. SNYMAN

59, D. RETIEF

60, M. FOREMAN

61, M. FOREMAN

62, J. R. DICKSON

63, V. PRINSLOO

64, A. SAUNDERS

OPPOSITE PAGE
65, S. LE ROUX

66, M. BRUWER

67, B. WILFORD

68. R. VISSER

69. S. INGERFELD

70. J. YOUNG

72, N. BRADFIELD

73, R. WILSON

74, R. MCKENZIE

75. M. GREGOR

76. C. GIAMPIETRI

77. K. CLOETE

79, J. VAN REENEN

80, S. LE ROUX

J. VAN NIEKERK

81, H. BRINK

82, J. R. WINCH

83, F. LE ROUX

84, F. LE ROUX

OPPOSITE PAGE
85, N. BRADFIELD

86, S. ADEY

09h00
12h00

As taxi drivers and traffic cops, vendors and miners, builders and doctors go about their work, the energy and vibrancy of South Africa reaches its peak. The wheels of industry are racing. The stock market groans under immense pressure. Cars pant at busy intersections while trains snake through the cities.

The land is overflowing with energy, exertion and effort but the serenity and tranquility of nature prevails. The beckoning hills mirror the golden laughter of the sun and flowers wave gracefully with the breeze's gentle touch. It is a rich wonderland of life – of wild mysterious beauty that captures your heart.

87, R. KLEVANSKY

88, M. BRUWER

OPPOSITE PAGE
89, H. ZANTMAN

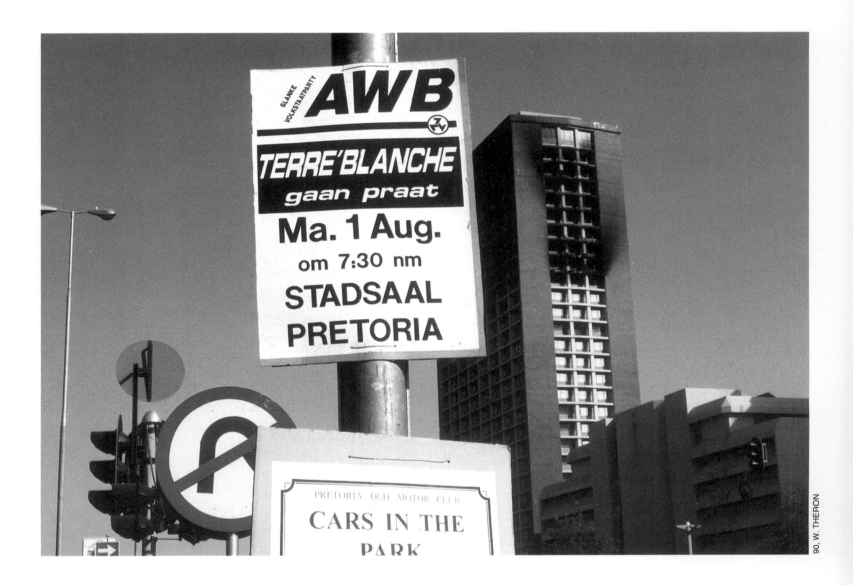

92. P. VICKERY

93. M. FOREMAN

94, I. THOMPSON

95, A. VAN DYK

96, T. COHEN

97, S. JEWELL

98, J. WARILOW

99, N. TRUTER

100. T. REDDY

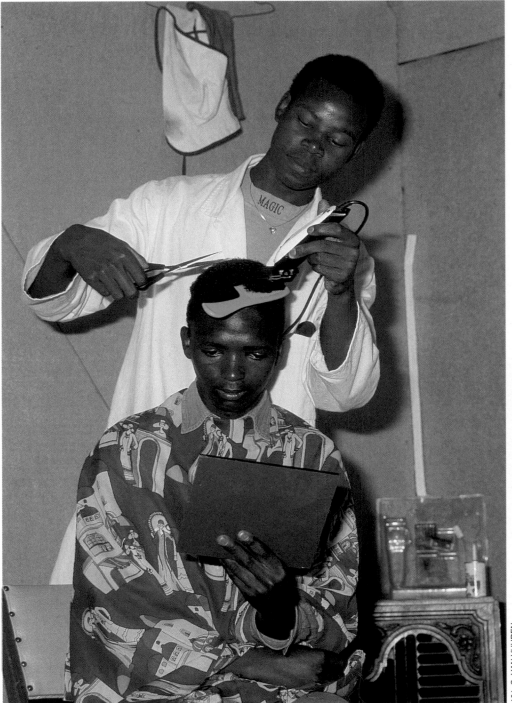

101, S. VAN VUUREN

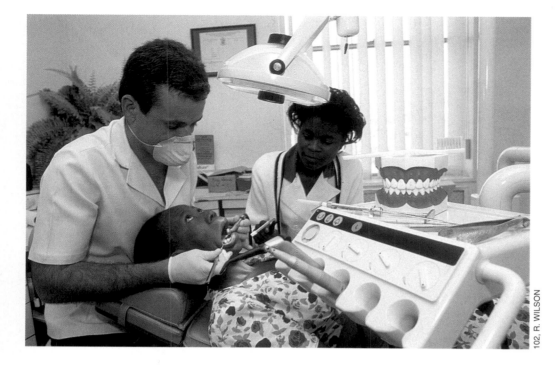

102. R. WILSON

103. B. LOUBSER

104, G. STRYDOM

105, C. ALBERTYN

106, P. HEADLEY

107, H. WILSON

108, S. JEWELL

109, B. BIGGS

110, K. HURNDALL

111, J. BAPTISE

112, M. DE WET

113, G. GERICKE

115, S. CHANCE

116, A. SEEGER

117, J. R. DICKSON

118, D. MURDOCK

OPPOSITE PAGE
119, P. DE WILZIN

120, M. LALLY

122, M. GREEN

123, C. THOMAS

OPPOSITE PAGE
124, L. GREENBERG

125, T. MOLLER

126, H. HATTING

RSAL

HT TO EQUALITY
EDOM FROM DISCRIMINATION

HT TO LIFE, LIBERTY
EDOM FROM SLAVERY
EDOM FROM TORTURE
T TO RECOGNITION
RE THE LAW
T TO EQUALITY BEFORE LAW
T TO LEGAL HELP
OM FROM ARBITRARY ARREST,
E AND DETENTION
T TO FAIR PUBLIC HEARING
TO BE INNOCENT UNTIL PROVEN,
Y
OM FROM INTERFERENCE WITH,
Y

T TO FREE MOVEMENT
TO ASYLUM IN OTHER,
TRIES
T TO NATIONALITY
T TO MARRIAGE AND FAMILY

DECLARATION OF HUMAN RIGHTS

RIGHT TO VOTE
FREE AND FAIR ELECTIONS
RIGHT TO OWN PROPERTY
FREEDOM OF BELIEF AND RELIGION
FREEDOM OF OPINION AND INFORMATION
RIGHT OF PEACEFUL ASSEMBLY AND ASSOCIATION
RIGHT TO FAMILY LIFE
RIGHT TO SOCIAL SECURITY
RIGHT TO WORK AND TO JOIN TRADE UNIONS
RIGHT TO REST AND LEISURE
RIGHT TO GOOD LIVING STANDARDS
RIGHT TO EDUCATION
RIGHT TO CULTURAL LIFE
GUARANTEE OF RIGHTS
DUTY TO COMMUNITY
HUMAN RESPONSIBILTY TO UPHOLD THESE RIGHTS

PLASCON

HUMAN RIGHTS FOR ALL

127, J. BRASSINNE

128, S. CHANCE

OPPOSITE PAGE
129, S. HURFORD

131, W. DEVOS

132, M. R. MOSS

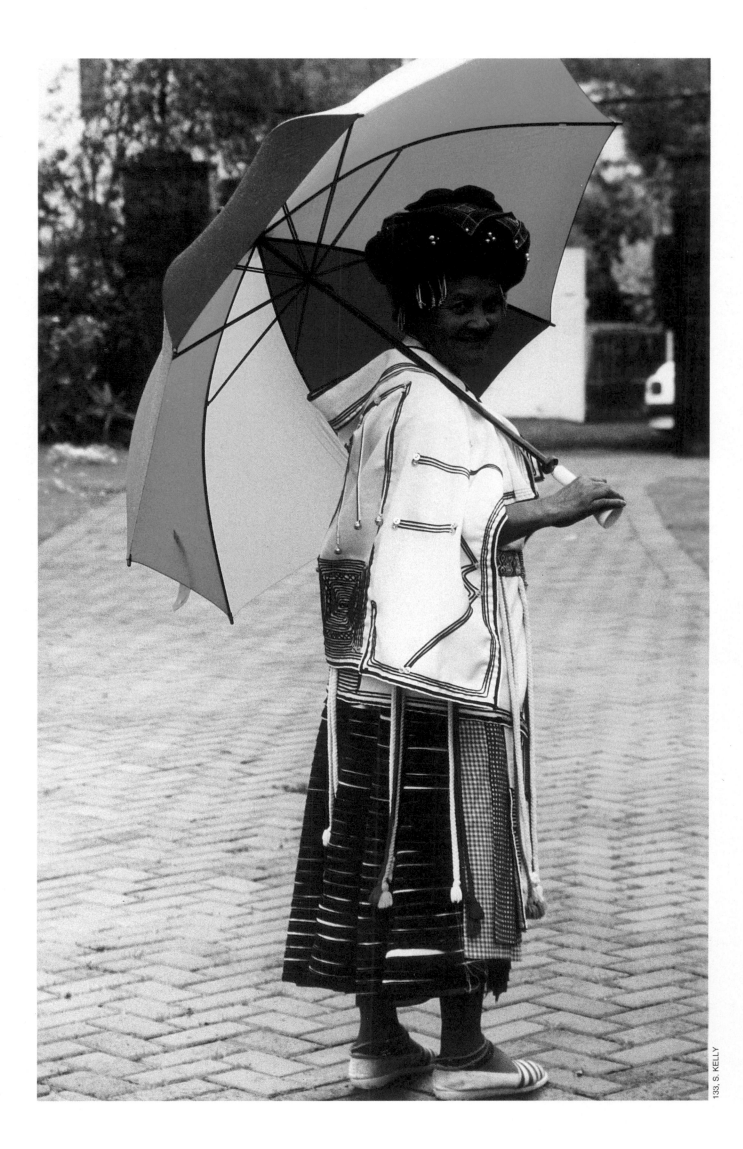

133, S. KELLY

134, E. WULFF

135, S. HURFORD

136. J. PERROTT

137, N. CREWDSON

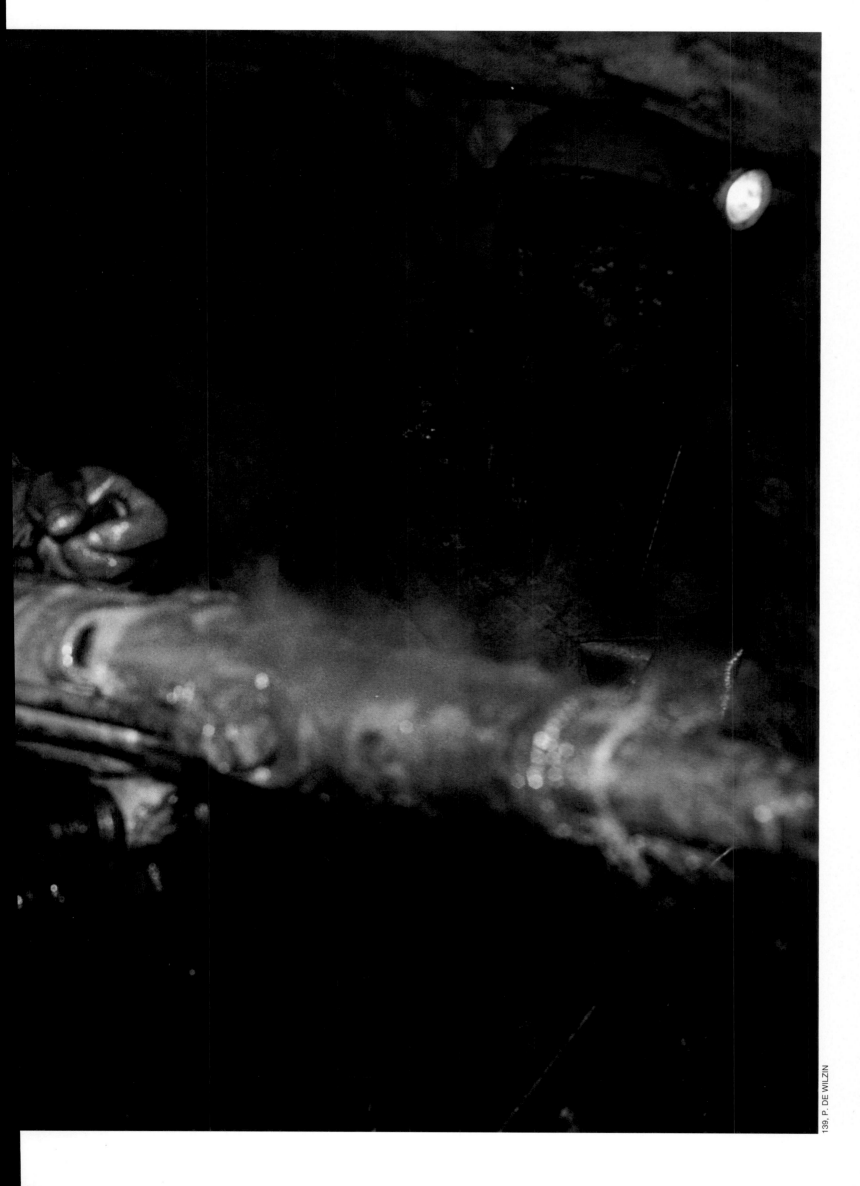

141, G. R. STUBBS

142, B. CLARKE

143, W. THORNLEY

144, S. GREAVES

145, B. THORNLEY

146, A. JANSEN

147, C. STANDER

148, A. MARTINUZZI

149, S. CHANCE

150, A OI WAGEN

151, A. MARTINUZZI

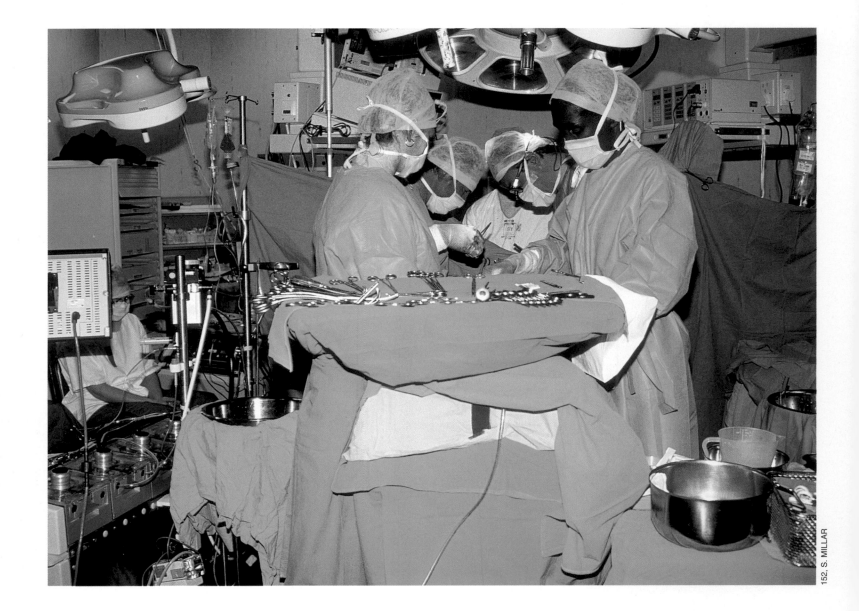

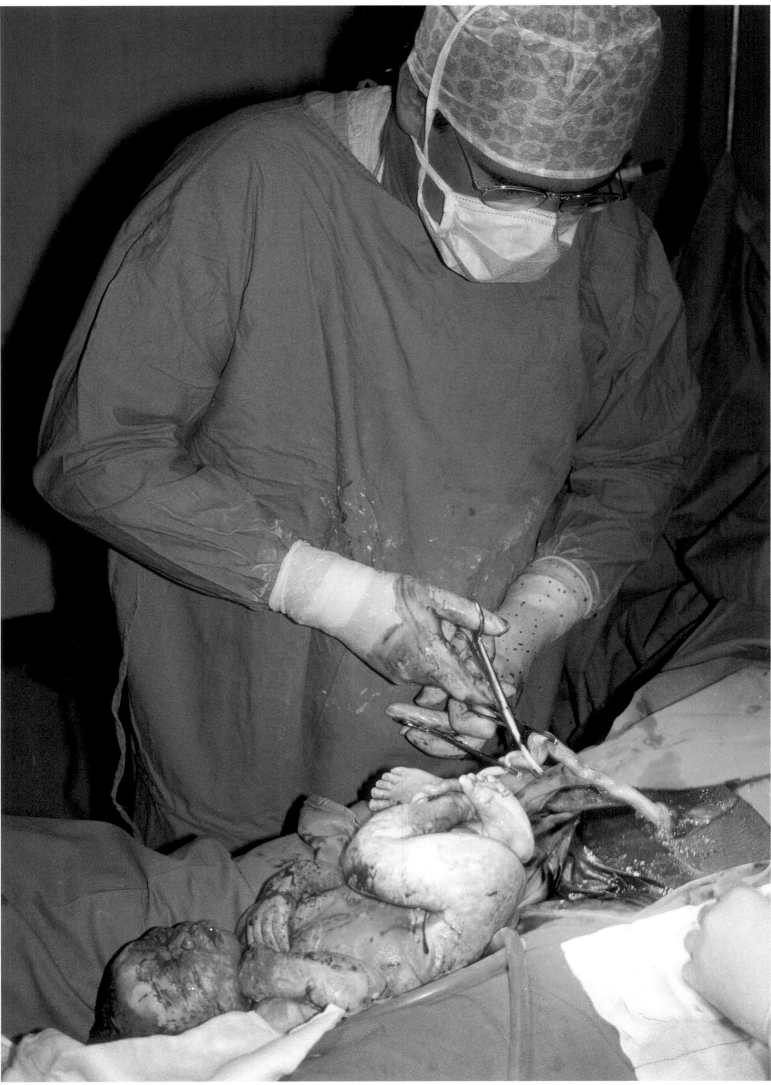

154, G. C. APSSA

155, E. MILLER

156, E. MARIA

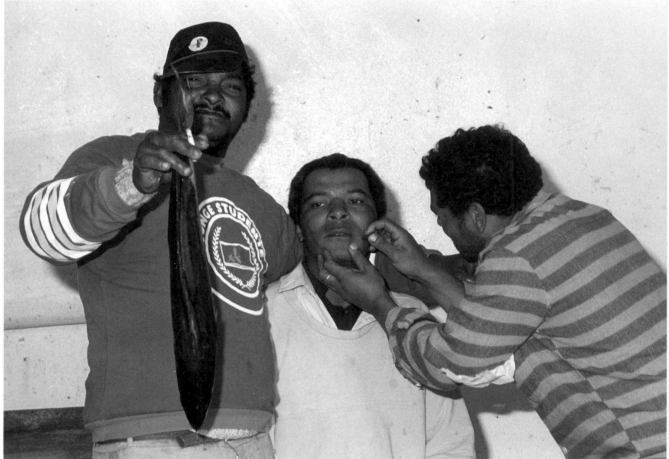

157, V. ROSSEAU

DIE WINKEL OP PATERNOSTER

158, M. BRUWER

OPPOSITE PAGE
159, R. KLEVANSKY

161, J. PERROTT

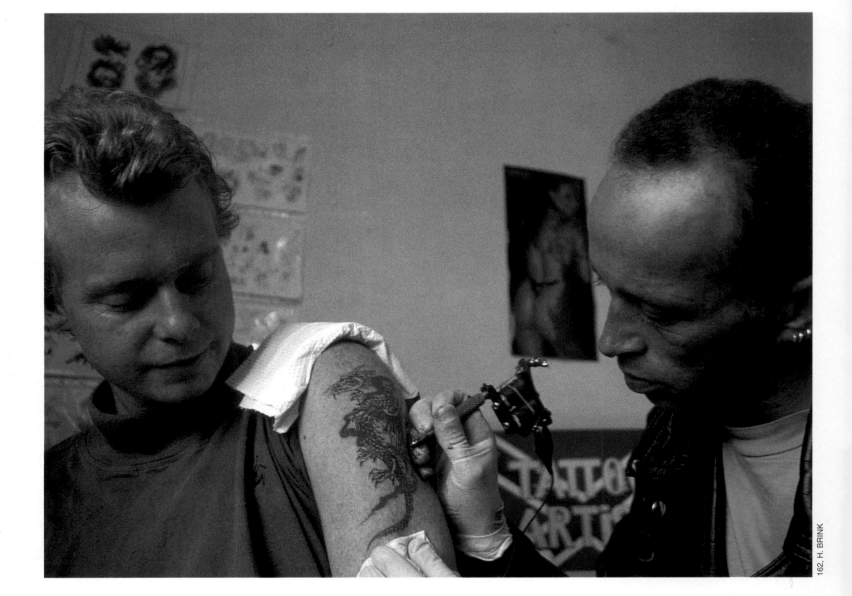

162, H. BRINK

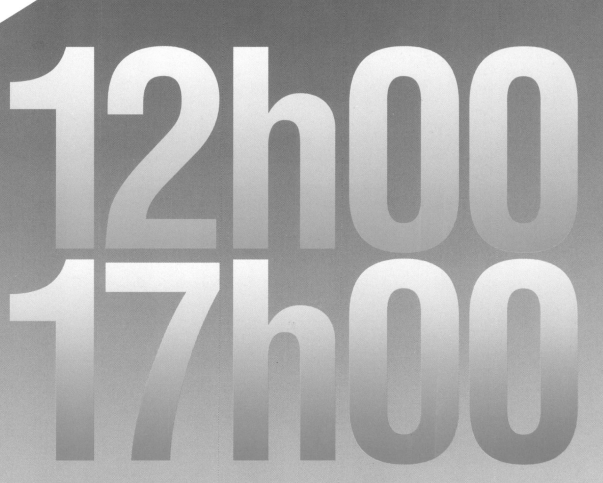

12h00
17h00

The South African midday sun beams down from an intense blue sky to reveal a land overflowing with colour, texture and beauty. A meadow fountain spray diffuses the sunlight into shimmering rainbows reflecting our kaleidoscopic nation.

Our afternoons are punctuated with various activities – children squander hours till homework time and breadwinners make the most of the last moments before closing time. As the wheels of industy grind to a halt, the wheels of transport pick up the rhythm. Weary commuters make their way home and the homeless begin their search for an unoccupied gutter, dustbin or drainpipe.

164, C. MEAD

165, H. ZANTMAN

166, V. ROSSEAU

167, S. CHANCE

168, A. S. WELZ

169, K. BOTHA

170, A. WELZ

NEXT PAGE
171, F. LOUW

172. D. ALLSCHWANG

173. B. ELOFF

174, J. KOPEC

176, N. BOTHMA

177, A. FLOQUET

178. S. ABBOTT

COUTURIER
DESIGNER
CREATIONS

179. T. MATTERSON

181, P. VICKERY

182, P. VICKERY

OPPOSITE PAGE
184, M. FOREMAN

183. J. URQUHART

185, F. DELY

186, F. DELY

189, R. MASON

190, L. CONNELLAN

192. B. THORNLEY

193, B. THORNLEY

194, D. REID

195, A. BISHOP-BOUCHER

196, K. BURNS

GEVAAR
VOLSTRUIS
EIERS MET
GIF BINNE

199, P. HEADLEY

200, W. OPENSHAW

201. S. JOHNSTON

202, S. STAUB

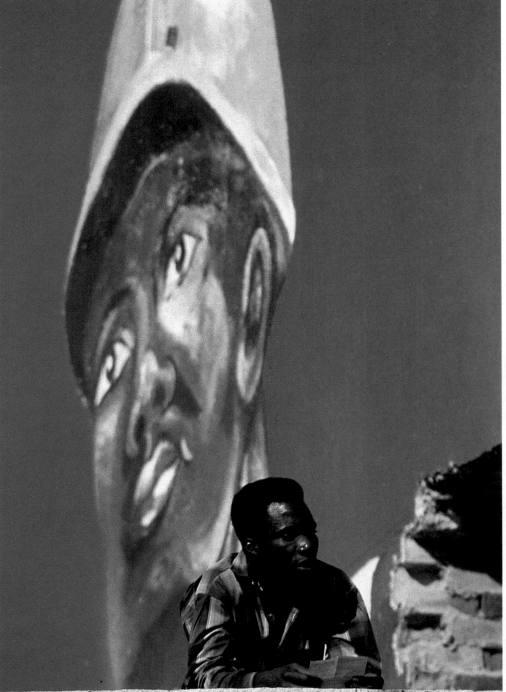

204, N. VAN NIEKERK

205, E. HEIDER

206, E. HEIDER

207, R. WILSON

208, K. RETIEF

209, C. ALBERTYN

210, S. LE ROUX

211, J. R. MCGREGOR

212, G. DE WET

OPPOSITE PAGE
214, C. STANDER

213, S. CHANCE

215, M. L. MYBURGH

217, B. THORNLEY

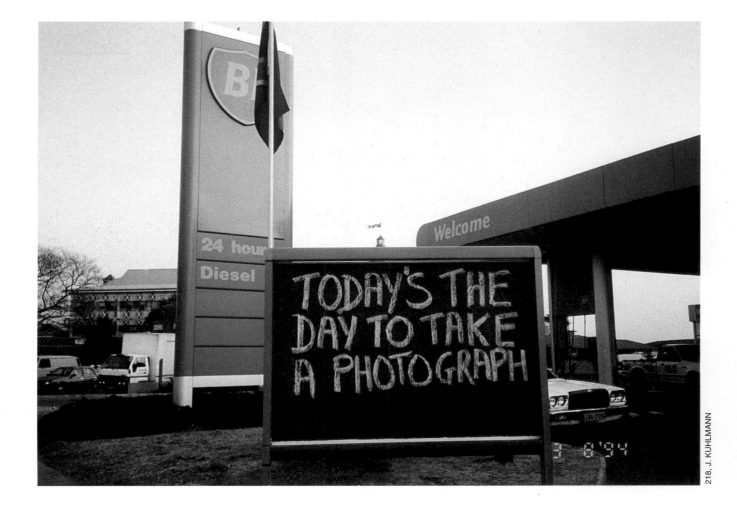

218, J. KUHLMANN

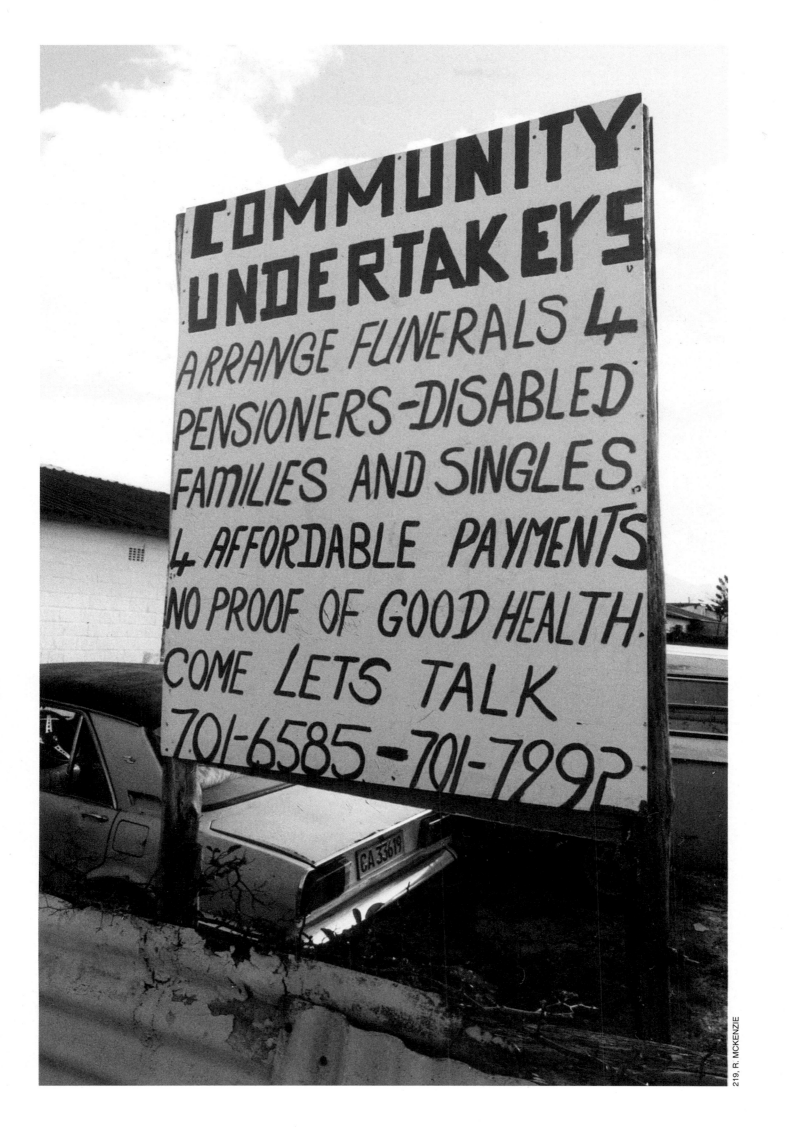

220, I. MULLER

222, M. STEYN

223, M. LANGFORD

224, J. R. DICKSON

225, B. ELOFF

226, M. NAPIER

227, R. DE VILLIERS

228, C. VORSTER

OPPOSITE PAGE
ABOVE: 229, S. DE KOCK

BELOW: 230, M. B. CUTHBERT

232, M. REEVES

231, A. PHITIOIS

233, L. WOLFAARDT

234, M. JOUBERT

236, D. R. CURRIE

237, S. CHANCE

238, J. KOPEC

239, G. VAN NIEKERK

240, E. WESSELS

242, M. LANGFORD

243. R. FORD

244. S. ABBOTT

245, N. OELOFSE

246, N. OELOFSE

247, N. KLOPPERS

248, N. KLOPPERS

249, S. CLARKE

250, T. REDDY

251, J. HULL

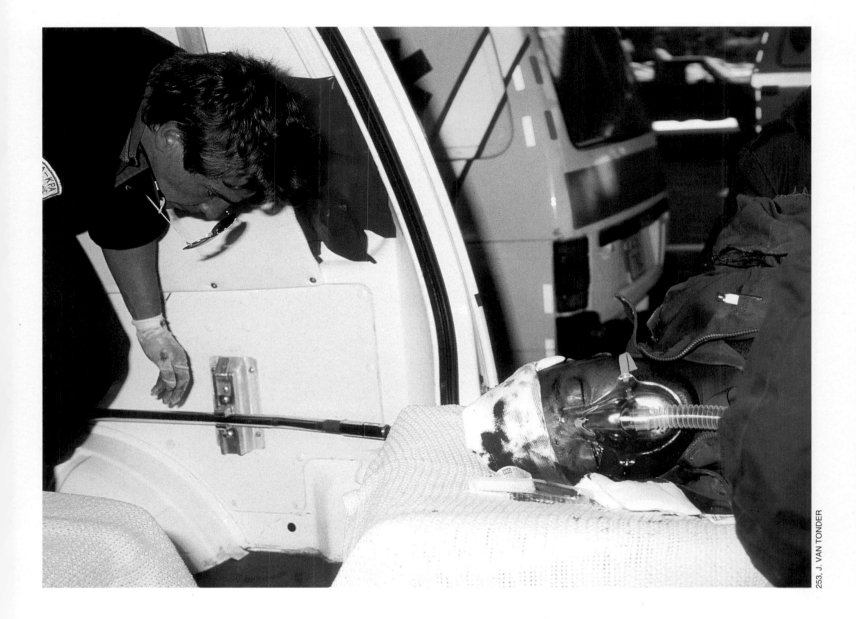

253, J. VAN TONDER

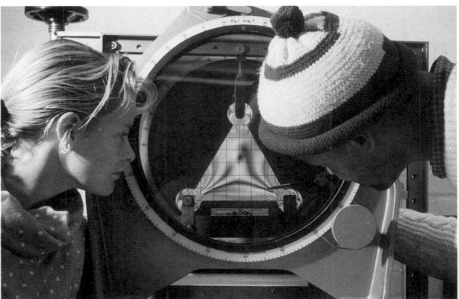

254, N. HOETS

256, D. HALL GREEN

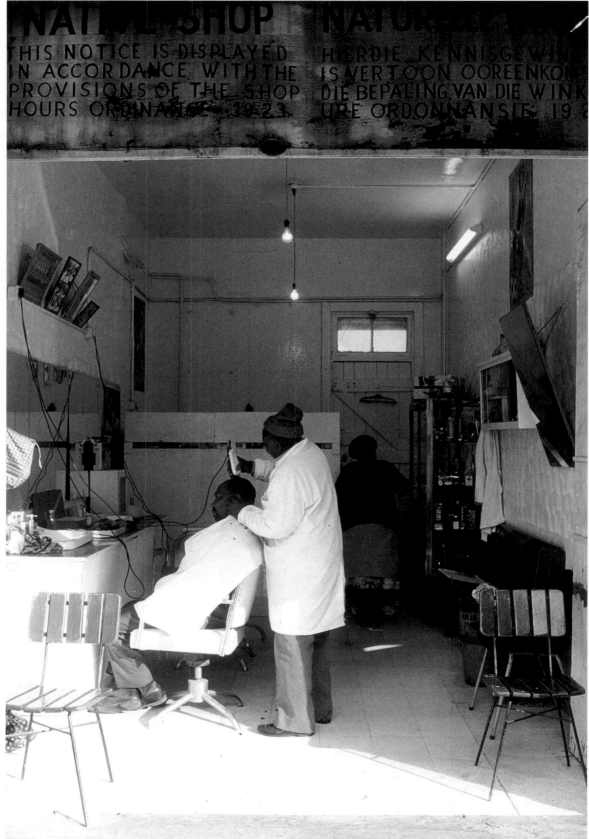

258. R. BOSHOFF

259, G. DE WET

260, G. DE WET

262. A. HETHERINGTON

264, C. BLOM

263, S. STAUB

266, R. MATTHEWS

267, R. SMITH

268, P. WULFSOHN

271, L. GREENBERG

270, R. FORD

272, D. DALLAS

273, M. OLIVER

274, L. CONNELLAN

275, F. BRANDL

276, E. VAN DEVENTER

277, G. DE WET

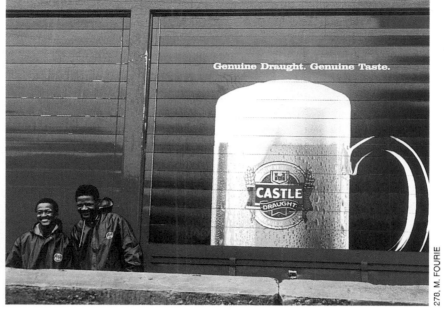

Genuine Draught. Genuine Taste.

CASTLE DRAUGHT

278, M. FOURIE

279, M. GREEN

280, P. A COQUI

281, R. BOSHOFF

282, R. FORD

283, K. BOTHA

284, R. WILSON

17h00
19h00

With the day's warmth still lingering in the land, the people of South Africa make their way home to their friends and families. As we go our separate ways, the diversity and contrast of our country is again unmistakable.

While some South Africans catch trains and taxi's, others motor in comfort. A last minute purchase at a vending stand or an item or two from a delicatessen rounds off another South African working day. It is time to prepare the evening meal, some by candlelight on wood-burning stoves while others pop instant meals into the microwave.

The last rays of light filter through the clouds, casting pastel shadows on our earth and sea.

287, F. SWANEPOEL

288, A. BAILEY

289, A. OLWAGEN

290. C. ATHERSTONE

292, P. SCHEDLER

293, S. REEVES

294, B. DU TOIT

295, A. OLWAGEN

296, G. VAN NIEKERK

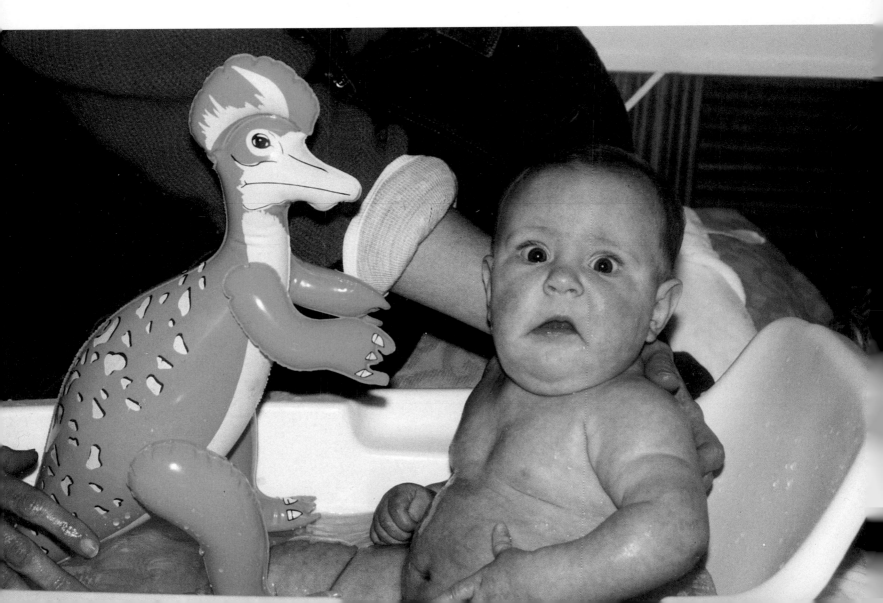

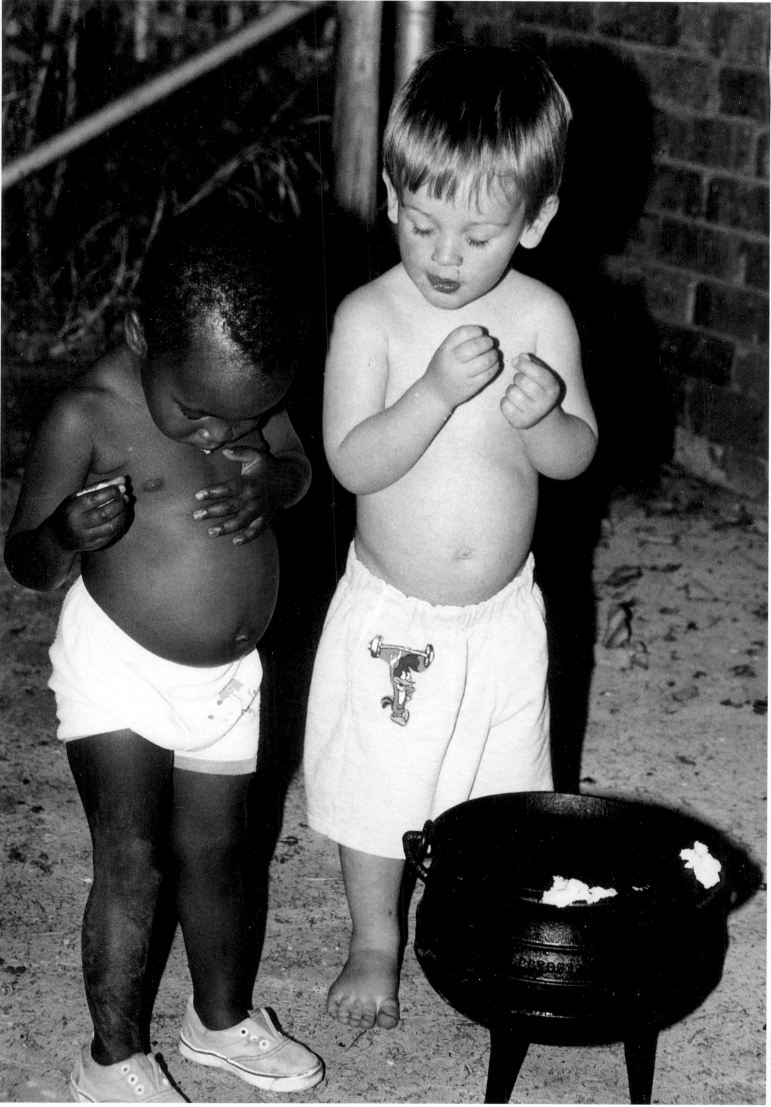

299, P. DE WILZIN

300, M. VAN DYK

301, C. VOLPERT

302, A. OLWAGEN

303, D. FUTERMAN

304, C. WATKINSON

000, K. DUNN

307, A. PHITIOIS

309, W. F. SILBURN

310, H. BRINK

311, A. VERCUEIL

313, D. G. GREAVES AIP

315, E. MARIA

310, S. CHANCE

314, D. BERKOWITZ

317, N. CREWDSON

318, M. FOREMAN

319, A. G. I. ORFANOS

320, J. BUNTMAN

321, J. BUNTMAN

322, N. BOTHMA

323, N. BOTHMA

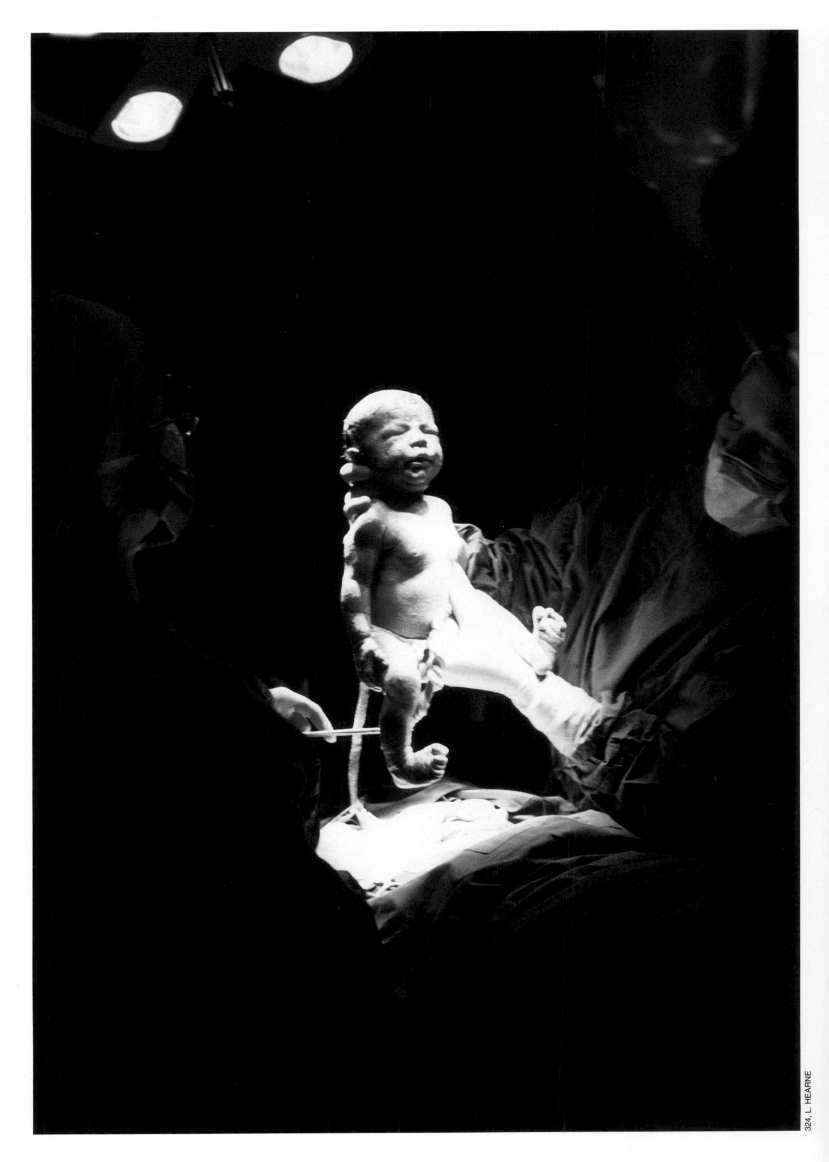

325, C. EVIAN

326, S. HARRY

327, C. STEVENSON

328, N. CREWDSON

329, R. FORD

330, C. BOTHMA

331, B. THORNLEY

332, J. GERLINGS

333, C. SNADDON

334, N. DE BLOCQ

335, R. MATTHEWS

336, R. VAN KERKHOF

337, D. G. GREAVES AIP

19h00
21h00

The marvellous colours of our panoramic sunsets are replaced by the amazing lights of man's intrepid handiwork, the darkness stitched by the purposeful glitter of electricity. The gentle glow of the television and the inertia of listening to canned music keeps many at home but others seek the frenetic activity of the bright lights and the haunting tones of the saxophone.

Bars, restaurants and shebeens, cinemas and theatres overflow in the nation's quest for entertainment, while some of our sport-loving nation are still playing under floodlights.

342, L. MEYER

345, B. KOPING

346, F. SWANEPOEL

347, A. G. I. ORFANOS

348. K. VISAGIE

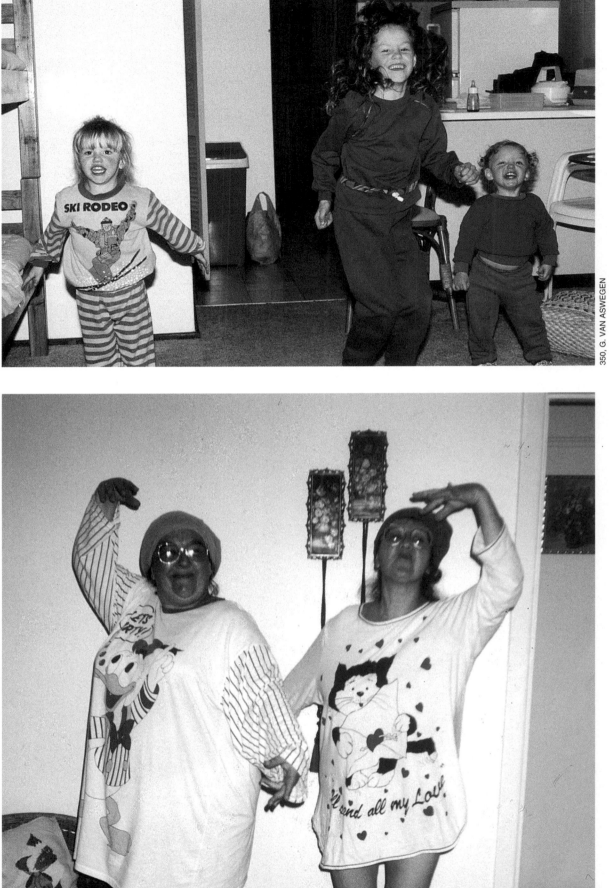

350, G. VAN ASWEGEN

351, R. LE GRANGE

352. M. LOON

353. E. HEIDER

354, M. TALJAARD

355, W. OOSTHUIZEN

356, S. CHANCE

357, W. THORNLEY

358. H. TOWEEL

359, C. CHANCE

360, R. PLISIC

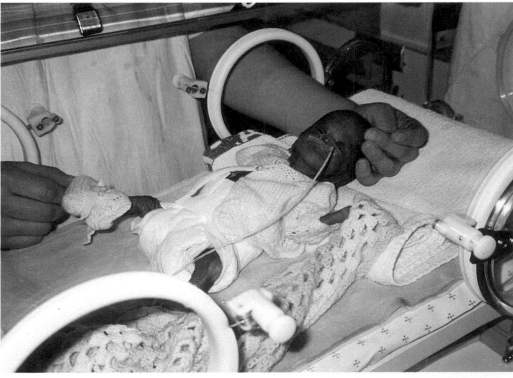

361, I. REINTEN

362, R. VAN ZYL

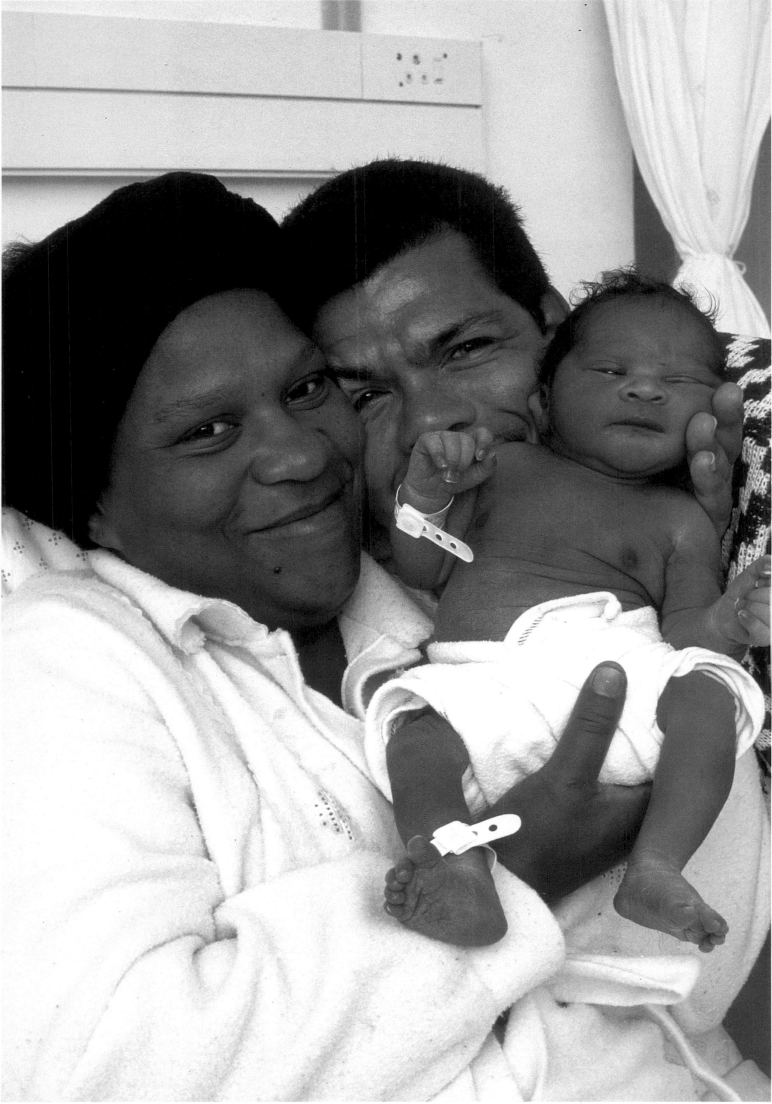

21h00
24h00

A reverential silence pervades as our country sleeps, enveloped by the stars. 3 August 1994, an extraordinary ordinary day, has come to an end. But, because an unobtrusive lens caught people as they really were, more was created than merely photographs. These images can be read as a diary of a journey into the very heart of our nation.

Photographers documented our daily lives, and gave us a glimpse into the unparalleled beauty and complexity of our country; into the wondrous harmony between people and land

The nightmares of yesterday are over and the dreams of a united tomorrow are materialising. Nkosi sikeleli Ningizimu Afrika. God bless South Africa.

366, E. MEYBERG

367, B. KOPING

368, E. MEYBERG

370, M. A. BROOMHEAD

371, C. A. HERBERT

372, H. HATTING

373. K. SCULLY

OPPOSITE PAGE
374, E. WELMANN

375, J. ROSSOUW

376, J. HOSSOUW

377, D. KENNING

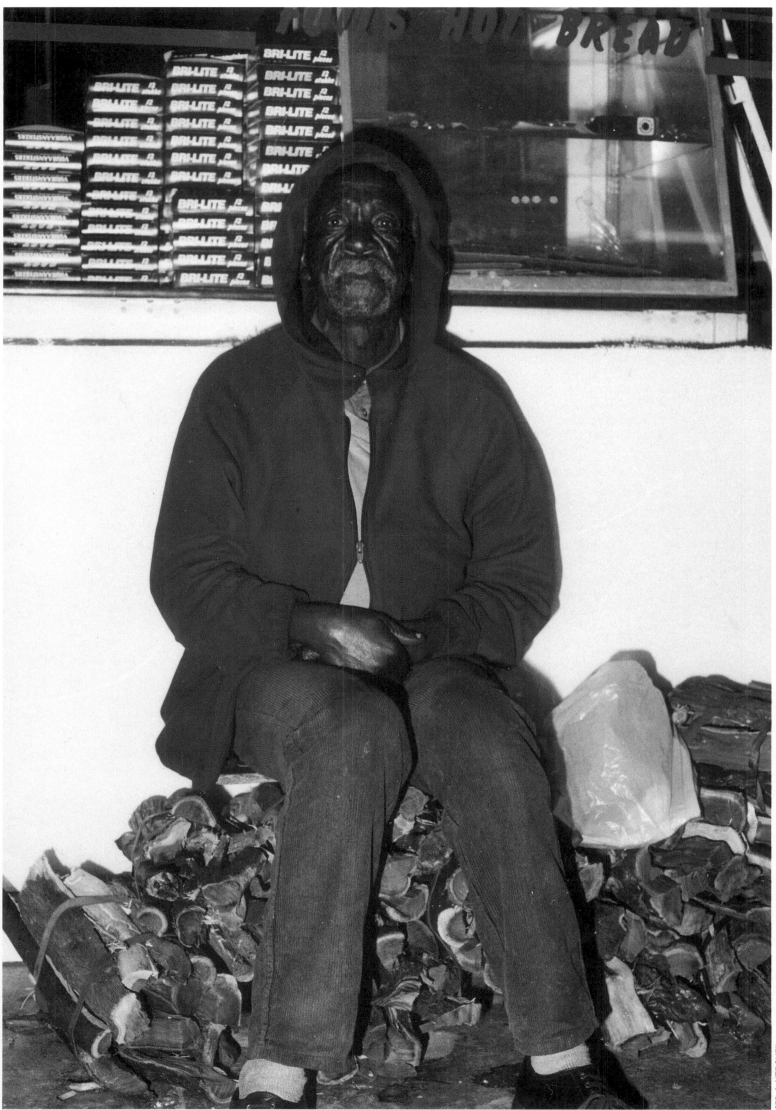

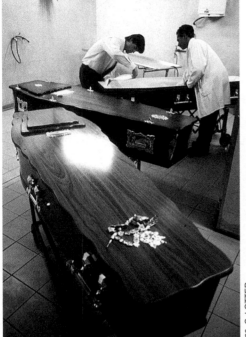

380, C. LOTTER

382, A. M. DE OLIVEIRA

SPECIAL
STORIES

Distressed Penguins

In the last days of June 1994, the Cape coast was hit by one of the worst oil disasters ever. More than seven and a half thousand hungry, miserable, distressed, oil-soaked penguins were brought to the doorstep of the South African National Foundation for the Conservation of Coastal Birds (SANCCOB).

Fighting against adverse weather conditions, hundreds of volunteers, bruised and bitten, fought desperately to save the lives of the penguins. Businesses and individuals gave generously, donating materials, offering assistance, and giving financial support.

Wingfield naval base and Ysterplaat airforce base took a load off SANCCOB's shoulders by accommodating a large number of birds. As a result of all these efforts, four thousand, four hundred birds were released. After the severe blow the penguin colony suffered, this is small consolation but it is the first step towards getting the colony back on its feet. It is tragic that nature has to suffer due to man's negligence and it is our responsibility to rectify the situation. Let us pray that such calamities can be avoided in the future.

LEFT: Hungry birds at the SANCCOB Centre, Milnerton, Cape Town.
PHOTO: KAREN JOOSTE

Ficksburg a Town at Peace

A mere 18 months ago Ficksburg was a town of terror - petrol bombs exploding, a child killed in a Border raid, people emigrating in droves and businesses closing down like ninepins, we even made CNN News frequently. Today Black, White, Indian, Chinese, Coloured and Portuguese children learn together happily. New shops are being built and new businesses are opening.

TESSA JOUGHIN

MAIN PHOTO: Rehabilitated jackass penguins from SANCCOB being released after the Apollo sea oil disaster at Silverstream, with John [...] photographing the event.
PHOTO: SHAWN BENJAMIN PHOTOGRAPHY

ABOVE: Dr Emmerson inoculating a jackass penguin for iron deficiency at SANCCOB.
PHOTO: SHAWN BENJAMIN PHOTOGRAPHY

[...]: Penguin in soapsuds.
PHOTO: SHAEN ADEY

Police dog goes missing after chase

EAST LONDON – A police dog went missing during a chase after three robbery suspects here yesterday.

The Border Police Liaison Officer, Lieutenant Colonel Garry Neuwenhuis, said members of the Dog Unit set up roadblocks after a Duncan Village resident had been robbed of goods to the value of R300 by three men early yesterday morning.

The suspects, allegedly travelling in a stolen bakkie, were spotted by Sergeant Henry Dixon and his partner, who gave chase.

The driver was forced off the road and the three suspects fled in different directions.

Sgt Dixon released his dog, Chaka, which set off in pursuit of one of the suspects.

Sgt Dixon followed close behind.

During the chase he came across a dagger and a balaclava lying in the grass.

Near a small ravine, a belt tied around a tree with the dog's chain was discovered.

The suspect and the dog could, however, not be found.

Anyone seeing Chaka, a seven-year-old black and tan Alsatian, should contact the dog unit at 462243 or 10111.

The dog is vicious and no attempt should be made to capture it. – DDR

DAILY DISPATCH 2 Aug 1994

Together again . . . Sergeant Henry Dixon with his dog Chaka.
Picture by MIKE KNOTT

PIC TAKEN 3RD AUG /APPEARED 4TH AUG
DAILY DISPATCH.

Chaka, handler reunited

Daily Dispatch Reporter

EAST LONDON — The police dog Chaka has been reunited with his anxious master after going missing for two days.

Chaka was found at K.C.W. Engineering in Magnolia Road, Braelynn, on Tuesday, by the owner, Mr Kingsley Wilmot, who arrived to discover him growling angrily at anyone who approached.

Mr Wilmot alerted the SPCA who informed the police. The dog handler, Sergeant Henry Dixon, was summoned.

"You should have seen the reunion; it was quite touching," Mr Wilmot said explaining how Chaka had bowled over an elated Sgt Dixon.

Sgt Dixon, who has had sleepless nights worrying about his dog, said he was relieved Chaka had been returned unharmed.

The dog went missing on Monday after he was set on the trail of a robbery suspect in Buffalo Flats.

Police later found the dog's chain tied to a tree. They surmised he had caught the suspect but the man had managed to slip his belt under the dog chain and used it to tie the animal to the tree and escape.

Captain André Grobbelaar of the dog unit said yesterday he believed Chaka had got loose and continued searching for the suspect.

The factory is several kilometres away from **where he was set loose.**

Caring and upright ▶

I have submitted two photographs of our enrolment of the Daxina Brownie Pack and Guide Company, which took place on the evening of the 3rd August, 1994. It was especially exciting as it heralded the start of Guiding in the Indian Community in Lenasia South. We are trying to encourage girls to join the Girl Guide Movement, which trains tomorrow's citizens to be caring and upright people.

THE FIRST PHOTO depicts the leaders of the Guide Company being enrolled. Mrs Jill de Villiers of Southern District is enrolling Vimla, Sally and Patt. The Brownies and Guides who had just been enrolled are saluting their leaders.

THE SECOND PHOTO was taken after the enrolment. Mrs Helen Norman is with some of the Guides.

The Association has always worked with girls of all colours and various religions. When people were talking about the new South Africa, one of my black Commissioners remarked that for us it isn't "new" as we have always worked together.

A week after our enrolment on the 3rd August, 1994, we enrolled 22 coloured girls in Ennerdale – another first for our Region. What a joy it is to see the eager young faces of these girls who enjoy the comradeship which Guiding gives them.

MRS L BRADLEY
TRANSVAAL
REGIONAL COMMISSIONER

◄ 'n Dag in die lewe van Suid-Afrika se blinde drieling

Wat het Suid-Afrika se enigste blinde drieling gedoen op Woensdag 3 Augustus? Ek het my kamera gevat en vir hulle gaan kuier.

Die blinde Strauss-drieling wat soveel opslae gemaak het in die media toe hulle vyf jaar gelede gebore is, het intussen half vergete geraak en woon nog al die jare saam met Ma Amanda, Pa Bart en nog twee ouer sussies in hulle pienk & grys huisie in Freemanstraat 11, Freemanville, Klerksdorp.

Toe ek daar aankom, was daar groot opgewondenheid, omdat Oupa Hannes Strauss van Orkney sou kom kuier – hulle is baie geheg aan hom, veral vandat Ouma onlangs dood is. Hy het kom help beplan aan die drieling se vyfde verjaarsdagpartytjie op 5 Augustus, twee dae later.

Stefanie, Sonja en Sylvia Strauss is al drie heeltemal blind, ondanks oogoperasies. Sonja is ook spasties en in 'n mate vertraag. In hierdie stadium is daar nie hoop dat hulle ooit sal kan sien nie; die ogies is besig om in die kaste terug te sak en hulle ondervind soms probleme met ingroeiende ooghaartjies en jeukende oogkaste.

Die drieling se ma, mev. Amanda Strauss, sê die drie is baie geheg aan mekaar en wanneer die een siek is, voel die ander twee dit aan en wil ook nie eet nie.

Hulle gaan soggens na die Janie Schneiderskool vir Gestremdes in Klerksdorp, maar wanneer hulle aanstaande jaar skoolgaande ouderdom bereik, sal hulle geskei moet word. Stefanie en Sylvia sal na 'n skool vir blindes gestuur word – waarskynlik die Prinshofskool in Pretoria – maar Sonja sal moet agterbly, omdat sy nie kan loop nie en spasties is.

Die drie blom wanneer hulle oupa in die nabyheid is. Hulle het ook 'n oppasser, Amelia van Zyl (18), wat wondere met hulle verrig en saam met hulle na die Janie Schneiderskool gaan om hulle te help met terapie en onderrig. Toe hulle kleiner was, het die huishulp, Lena, hand bygesit het met hulle versorging. Hulle is ook baie geheg aan hulle twee ouer sussies, wat in die laerskool is.

Amanda sê sy en haar man Bart het eers vier weke ná die drieling se geboorte agtergekom dat hulle blind is en dit was vir hulle 'n geweldige skok. Die drie pas egter goed aan en is veral lief vir musiek. Dit gaan verder goed met hulle gesondheid en hulle ontvang gereeld fisioterapie.

Hulle klasonderwyseres wat reeds die afgelope drie jaar met hulle werk, mev. Jobie Wentzel, sê die drietjies is baie goed aangepas in die skool en kommunikeer goed met die ander kinders. Hulle herken al die stemme van die onderwyseresse en hulle klasmaats. Hulle ander sintuie is baie goed ontwikkel.

Hoewel daar 'n trustfonds bestaan, is dit byna uitgeput en Pa Bart sê hy weet nie wat gaan hy maak as hulle na spesiale skole gestuur moet word nie.

Suid-Afrika se enigste blinde drieling is nie vergete nie en ons hoop dat meer mense aan hulle sal dink wanneer hulle blaai in "A Day in the Life of the New South Africa".

**ALTA PRETORIUS
KLERKSDORP**

A man I met ►

As someone who participated in the happening more than ten years ago with some very fond memories, I felt that I was somehow part of the 3rd of August 1994 as well. It just wouldn't have seemed right if I had let the day go by without taking at least one picture. I decided to take the day as it came and look for my pictures from any opportunity that presented itself. When selecting my pictures some three weeks later from those that I had taken, I was reminded of some of the harsh realities of life in South Africa – and some good ones – and decided to write about them as part of my entry.

This is the story of a man I met at the Keg & Crown in Oxford Road, Rosebank, at lunchtime. He introduced himself as Jesse James from Citylab and offered to process all the film I had shot for free, as his contribution to the Day. I photographed him at about 3pm on a customised Yamaha on the pavement of the Keg & Crown, trying to highlight the contrast between the man in a suit and this gleaming red, silver and gold-plated machine. You could have knocked me down with a feather when, two weeks later at Citylab, I learnt of his tragic death the day before. When I related the story of what Jesse had done on the 3rd, and that I had a photograph of him, the asked to print the picture, which

they gave to his wife at the funeral in remembrance of him.

**FRANS DELY
BRYANSTON**

Well-known character

Mandla is a well-known character around the Durban yacht basin, where he earns his living diving under the yachts and cleaning their bottoms. He also crews on yachts and legend has it that, one day, he went out on one very large boat, thinking they were going out just for the day but, on enquiring as to the destina tion, he was informed "Cape Town". T news didn't upset him in the least an so Mandla went to Cape Town.

**D H SELLARS
DURBAN NORTH**

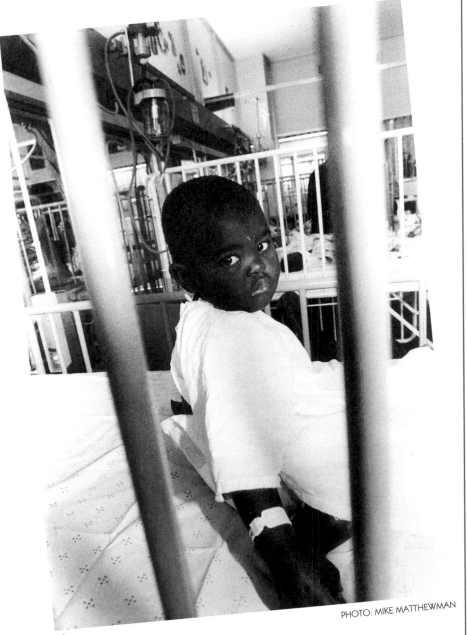

PHOTO: MIKE MATTHEWMAN

▲ Abandonded baby Londi hoping and waiting for the new South Africa

PIETERMARITZBURG – Anyone who has information about the above missing child, who calls herself Londi, is requested to contact social workers at Grey's Hospital at this number: 458 181 ext 136. The Townhill police found her with a broken leg. She is about two years old.

Kucelwa onolwazi ngalomntwana owatholwa ngamaphoyisa aseTownhill ukuba athintane nophiko losonhlalakahle esibhedlela iGrey's Hospital. Lentombazanyane eyatholwa iphuke umlenze wesokunxele eneminyaka elinganiselwa kwemibili, ithi inguLondi. Inombolo yocingo yasesibhedlela ithi 458 181 ext 136.

The Andrew family ▶

Our son and his family – Robert and Estelle and their two children, John-Paul and Natasha. In the new South Africa, they now live with confidence and dignity – AT LAST.

**BOSKY ANDREW
CONSTANTIA**

Die wat sien en nie sien nie

Op drie Augustus is my neef, Re (45), begrawe en sy oom ds Bey Naudé het die diens waargeneer voorgelees uit die Bybel: "…ons gered in hoop; maar die hoop w gesien word, is geen hoop nie; wat iemand sien, waarom hoop dit nog? Maar as ons hoop wat nie sien nie, dan wag ons daaro volharding." (Rom 8:24-25) By d graf is Gesang 353:4 gesing: "Ek aan wie'k my toevertrou het, al dan dag en nag".

**ELSA VERLOREN VAN THEMAAT
KAAPSTAD**

Rotary Exchange Scholar from Indiana, USA

Hello, my name is Christopher Lane, and I am currently studying in South Africa on a Rotary Youth Exchange Scholarship. My home is in Indiana, in the US.

The reason for this letter is that, in the States there is a ten-hour time difference from South Africa and, because of this difference, my camera date says it was taken on the 2nd, when truthfully the pictures were taken on the 3rd.

I think the whole idea of the book is wonderful and I hope the confusion won't eliminate my pictures from the contest.

CHRISTOPHER LANE
PORT ELIZABETH

"It's a dog's life"

These pictures of our 6-month old Bernese Mountain dogs have two purposes for your book.

1. As you can see, they always adopt the same pose and posture, therefore they will make perfect book-ends for your famous book.

2. They are brown, black and white in about the same proportions as our South African population. These colours have their own wonderful brilliance and together they make up a magnificent and beautiful beast. *That's* how the new South Africa will be.

B ANDREW
CAPE TOWN

Strength and health through food

Here are photo's which I hope will represent the new South Africa. They were taken at Durbanville taxi-rank, where our church has set up a soup kitchen on most week nights. Most of the people that you see here sleep in the bush, even during winter. The soup in the evenings is, for many of them, the only hot food that they receive in a day.

We hope in the future to start a night shelter, providing warm beds and safe surroundings.

The photo's were taken with Fujicolor 400.

**J L GERRETSEN
CAPE TOWN**

This boy lets go of the saddle and reins for the first time under the thrilled and watchful eyes of his helper

Laughs and Smiles

Thanks for organising this wonderful opportunity to show South Africans — heart and soul!

I found a moving subject and was thrilled that they were happy to let me photograph them!

The SA Riding for the Disabled gives people with all sorts of disabilities chances to experience the thrill of horse-riding.

The helpers and teachers all work as volunteers and swear the laughs and smiles are magnificent rewards!

Watching the pupils (some riding for the first time) was a moving experience.

Blind people also ride here but had no classes on 3 August.

It's great to have had a day to see South Africa moment by moment with a view to capturing the seconds permanently.

Whether you can use these pics or not — thanks for the great work you're doing!

**ALISON PLACE
CLAREMONT**

PS: The horses too are amazing — carefully chosen with ever-patient temperaments.

In the stable with the pony he rides

Rose-Act Study Centre, Alexandra Township

An old bus that has been converted into a study centre in Alexandra Township.

CHRISTINE KEYTE

Marietjie and Dimple

Fully appreciating the fact that the proceeds will go to the South African National Council for the Blind, I thought I would like to send in this photo of my blind friend, Marietjie Coetzee, who is a telephonist at the Standard Bank (Rustenburg) and every day walks a good few blocks to work – with her wonderful guide-dog Dimple helping her to negotiate a railway crossing safely. Unfortunately, while deciding the best way to take the photo, neither of us realized the train was about to leave the nearby station. Marietjie and Dimple were on one side of the railway line and I was on the other. Suddenly, the train appeared and all I managed was to shout to Marietjie to stand back for safety. The train rolled by and I only managed to get its tail end and Marietjie and Dimple looking relieved – not a great photo but I am pleased to support a great cause.

FAY, MARIETJIE AND DIMPLE
RUSTENBURG

▲ "Mina Mynah"

This means "my Mynah" in Zulu. Our tame Indian Mynah loves our maid, Grace, and follows her everywhere.

E D BILLES
GLENASHLEY

Some kids from Duncan Village near East London enjoyed a funride from Mr V Nkonyeni a builder from Fein-Boss.

PHOTO: M MNYAKAMA

Enigste oorblywende Siamesie is opgespoor

Die Siamese tweelingdogtertjies wat in Julie 1994 gesterf het nadat hulle die skeidingsoperasie nie kon oorleef nie, het medici en die publiek laat wonder oor die welstand van die enigste oorlewende Siamesie in Suid-Afrika. Sy het egter van die mediese toneel en mediafokus verdwyn en min mense was bewus van waar sy haar bevind.

Navrae het aan die lig gebring dat Mpho Mathibela tans in Jouberton, Klerksdorp se swart dorp, woon en nou sewe jaar oud is.

Die hele wêreld is in 1988 aangegryp deur die Siamese tweeling Mpho en Mponyana Mathibela wat suksesvol van mekaar geskei is tydens 'n operasie van sewe uur in die Baragwanath Hospitaal. Mpho was die sterker een van die twee. Haar sussie Mphonyana was blind en doof na die operasie en het twee jaar later, in 1990, gesterf.

Mpho se stryd om te oorleef en aan te pas, het almal aangegryp. Haar mediese behandeling en nasorg het byna R1,5 miljoen gekos en 'n spesiale "Mathibela Trustfonds" is in die lewe geroep om haar moeder, Sophie, by te staan met die uitgawes. (Haar pa het hom uit die voete gemaak direk na die geboorte van die Siamese tweeling).

Die voorsitster van die Mathibelafonds is mev Maggie Nkwe, vrou van Biskop David Nkwe van die Anglikaanse Kerk, wat feitlik die hele Noordwes-provinsie bedien. Hulle woon tans in Flamwood, Klerksdorp.

Die fondse het egter opgedroog namate die publiek se belangstelling vervaag het. Mpho het nou skoolgaande ouderdom bereik en is opgeneem in die Tiangskool in Jouberton. Haar onderwyser, mej Kukie Jilimba, sê Mpho het na haar mening eintlik spesiale onderrig nodig, maar daar is geen spesiale skole in die omgewing nie.

Mev Nkwe wat as voog optree teenoor Mpho, sê Mpho se mediese toestand is nie onlangs geëvalueer nie omdat die fondse uitgeput is. Hulle is dus nie seker of sy spesiale onderrig benodig nie. Sy kom normaal voor, verstaan wat aan haar gesê word en het 'n redelike woordeskat. Sy het effense koördinasieprobleme met haar een hand en sy loop mank. Sy raak soms gefrustreerd as sy nie alles kan doen wat haar maats kan doen nie, maar is vriendelik en gewild onder haar medeskoliere.

ALTA PRETORIUS
KLERKSDORP

BEHIND THE SCENES
'A Day in the Life of the New South Africa'

The magic of the project, 'A Day in the Life of the New South Africa' began for me the moment I paged through the previous book. The pictures moved me – I laughed and cried as I experienced 26 May 1982, a day frozen in time. As I read the story behind the project an excitement welled up in me and thoughts and ideas flooded my mind. The project simply had to be repeated and with the birth of our new nation the timing would be perfect.

Dr Rowland, my dedicated team consisting of Heather Nel, Janessa Urquhart and Heather Waite and I worked tirelessly, planning and laying the groundwork for the project that would touch the hearts and lives of thousands of South Africans.

For a project such as this one to succeed, powerful media partnerships are needed. Consequently the first call was made by Dr Rowland to one time adversary and now great friend Quentin Green, Chief Executive: Television, at the SABC. His response was one of immediate enthusiasm. We were elated, the project *was* going to be a success.

Meetings were held with Kobus Schoeman, Programme Manager: GMSA and his efficient and talented team and the first thoughts and plans were set in motion. Lengthy and heated debates regarding a suitable date for 'the day' were held. "Should it be a day in Spring, should it coincide with the opening of Parliament, how soon after the election should it be staged?" Eventually, as with the previous project, it was decided that an absolutely ordinary day should be chosen – and so Wednesday 3 August 1994 came to be 'A Day in the Life of the NEW South Africa.'

The first floor in the Optima Services Building of the SANCB's headquarters in Pretoria became a hive of frenzied activity. Action lists were designed, press releases written and countless phone calls made (especially by chatterbox, Janessa). The previous 'Day in the Life' team were contacted to help and guide us.

During our first democratic election (28 April 1994), Dr Rowland and I were fortunate enough to find Colin Hall in his Johannesburg office. The joy and hope from the previous election day had left us all with a feeling of exultation and euphoria and together we shared our visions for the new South Africa. The coming together of our nation had given us all the emotional boost we needed. Colin Hall accepted the position of Patron of the project and in a first thoughtful gesture he wrote to business colleagues, asking them to join us in this venture.

The result was core funding to cover expenses for the project from CERES FRUIT GROWERS, SOUTH AFRICAN BREWERIES, CALTEX, OLD MUTUAL, and SAPPI. WOOLTRU, of which Colin Hall is Chairman, also contributed generously.

Other core sponsors who later joined the project included FUJI, and Hylton Appelbaum of the LIBERTY LIFE FOUNDATION again extended a hand of friendship. These partners enabled us to print entry forms, order forms and to prepare and execute advertising campaigns without dipping into scarce resources.

Not only did Colin Hall bring much needed funding and prestige to the project but our 'special dad' also gave us a belief in our own abilities which enabled us to reach new heights.

Di Pieterse,
Bob Thornley, Vanessa Bouwer, Janessa Urquhart, Angie Bailie,
Heather Nel and William Rowland (seated).

Our search for previous team members continued and the effervescent Di Pieterse was the next person we were to meet. Di, who had worked for the SANCB at the time of the previous project, and who is now a well-established business woman, screamed with delight at the prospect of the new project. Our search was complete, but for one, and Bob Thornley (affectionately known as the weasel) was the final member of the team. He immediately frightened us to death with stories of the immensity of the project but his enthusiasm and contagious sense of humour soon had 'the team', as he called us, rearing to go. His own dedicated staff Giulio and Angie immediately became part of the team and Bob accepted the position of Chief Judge.

The TEAM was in place. As we met with prospective partners we realised how the success of the previous project had opened doors for us and for this we're very grateful to the 1982 team.

With the television partnership with GMSA secured, other media partnerships were next on the agenda. Dr Rowland and Heather met with Goven Reddy, Chief Executive: Radio and as with his television counterpart his support was immediate and substantial. Follow up discussions with Raymond Schenk, Executive Manager SABC and long time friend of the SANCB resulted in public service announcements in seven languages, thus ensuring that all communities knew of our project. Interviews on all radio stations added momentum to the success of the project. Koos Radebe, Station Manager of Radio Metro was just as supportive and interviews, adverts and announcements followed.

We then visited, Ken Owen, Editor of the Sunday Times. I was a little nervous particularly as I was an admirer of Ken Owens' outstanding writing ability but my nerves were unfounded as he was warm and supportive and the ensuing partnership with his colleague Ireen Spicer, Assistant Editor Special Projects, was very meaningful.

Support to the project from all members of the media was phenomenal and the SANCB would like to acknowledge the vital role played by the media. Without you the project may not have succeeded. I must also admit that when Arnand Naidoo and Jane Hicks clicked their cameras on the 8 o'clock news on 2 August I leapt off the couch with joy.

Other partnerships were still to be cemented and these included the relationship with the CNA. A first meeting with Ian Outram, Managing Director, Peter Moore, Geoff Cooper and Wilma Guest led to a very productive partnership. CNA played a crucial role in all stages of the project. They carried our entry forms, staged in-store promotions, distributed the book (at no profit to themselves) and generally provided us with expert advice and much needed encouragement.

CNA also brought two other vital partners into the project and these were our photographic partner FUJI AND TRANS SA BOOK DISTRIBUTORS. Norman Dick, Marketing Manager of Fuji added a special quality to the project and he and his team pulled out all the stops to make this project the success it has been. Glenda Parker, Managing Director of TSABD ensured that the book would be available at all other book stores nationwide.

An extra special partner has to be SAPPI who, like with the previous project provided us with 100 tons of paper at cost price. The book is printed on the superb SHAKA GLOSS paper manufactured by SAPPI FINE Papers. We are grateful to all at SAPPI who made this magnificent donation possible, particularly, Johan van Wyk, Charles Combrink and Martin Chauke.

Des and Dawn Lindberg added a touch of glamour to the previous project and they dazzled again this time. A spectacular celebrity launch of 'A Day' was staged at the Civic Theatre at their renowned production of Godspell. Des wrote a moving song which was performed by the Godspell cast and of course Des & Dawn themselves. The Celebrity Launch was a fitting way to initiate this project as it was an evening filled with fun, laughter and energy. The celebrities that arrived sparkled and were very gracious as they were 'shot' by fellow guests armed with cameras.

SATOUR have been wonderfully supportive and visits to Dr Ernie Heath have resulted in positive steps being taken in the use of the book as a marketing tool in attracting foreign visitors to our shores. A very encouraging letter from Minister de Villiers was also greatly appreciated.

We wanted people to participate in the project because they wanted to and not because they were motivated by prizes, nonetheless we wanted to reward the photographers with fabulous prizes. Di, with her wealth of experience and contagious enthusiasm secured valuable prizes for our winners.

The prize for the cover picture was a ticket for two to any destination in the world sponsored by our own SOUTH AFRICAN AIRWAYS with R10 000 spending money from the LIBERTY LIFE FOUNDATION.

SOUTHERN SUN provided a spectacular South African dream holiday in the Presidential Suites of 3 of their top hotels viz. The Cape Sun, Beverley Hills and Bongani Sun.

SAA, COMAIR AND BUDGET RENT-A-CAR added all the domestic travel. SOUTHERN SUN also sponsored a sumptuous partners breakfast and accommodation for the team. Generous prizes were also received from MOUNTAIN SHADOWS MANOR HOUSE, THE CONSERVATION CORPORATION AND ZULU NYALA GAME LODGE.

3 August was spent the way it should have been and all members of the team took pictures of course. Janessa, Heather and I together with the GMSA team visited places of interest in Pretoria, Johannesburg and the surrounding areas. We met beautiful people, poor people, angry people and desperate people. I was particularly moved by the homeless people we met at the Johannesburg Station who welcomed us into their tiny, fragile homes. I found it difficult to take photographs of their lives, – it seemed like such and invasion.

Thereafter almost within a kilometre or two we drove through some plush suburbs of Johannesburg and one could only but be struck by the contrasts and diversity of our land. Our day ended at the De Wildt Cheetah Research Centre where again one was touched by the beauty and vitality of South Africa.

The judging of the more than 16 000 photographs was an enormous task and our judges Bob Thornley, Dawn Lindberg, Di Pieterse, Peter Stuckey, Joe Myburgh and myself were encouraged by the sense of optimism that emerged through the photographs. The flag was featured very prominently and so too the informal sector. It was also a privilege to have photographs of our President, Nelson Mandela. An exhausting weekend was experienced but the judges were unanimous in their opinion that at least 3 books could have been compiled from photographs received.

The project has been a 'magical' experience because so many people have given of their time, energy and money. The entire staff of the SANCB pledged time in a variety of ways. Some joined the photographic team, or the data capturing, catering, exhibitions or general teams. Long hours were worked as staff joined to made the project a winning one. To the team leaders Sonya Smith, Chris Schutte, Marina Clarke, Niresh Singh and Annatjie Terblanche, I give my heartfelt thanks. To Pieter Lombard, André Kleynhans and Johan Grové I offer my congratulations for a truly superb computer programme that enabled us to capture the many thousands of photographs accurately. It was a wonderful experience to work with people that gave their all.

The affiliates of the SANCB also added to the prestige and success of the project and in particular the S A Guide Dog Association participated enthusiastically. It was also very gratifying to receive entries that reflected the work done by our affiliates.

This book is a splendid collection of photographs of our unique and vibrant country. I would like to thank Peter Stuckey and Wendy Matthews for adding their very special design talent to the project and for the magnificent book we have. Thanks also to Abdul Amien for his unique artistic touch with regard to the typography. Andrew Dodd and Simon Trace, Senior Executive TV1 Promotions have helped a great deal in the marketing of our book. CTP Book Printers have also created a superb final product and we acknowledge each person who played a part in the printing process particularly Hendrik van Rooyen.

The greatest reward has undoubtedly been the fact that the project will touch the lives of the people that will never see the book – the blind people of our country. To each person that has purchased a book I would like to say a big thank you for helping to make it possible to make a difference in the lives of blind and partially sighted people.

This project has been a fund-raisers dream and it has been a privilege to lead it. My special thanks go to Dr Rowland, Janessa Urquhart, Heather Nel, Heather Waite, Linda Rijneke, Colin Hall, Bob Thornley, Di Pieterse, Michael Johnson, all the sponsors, contributors, my husband Peter (for his patience) to my family and friends and to the South Africans who joined with us to make this project so SPECTACULAR.

Vanessa Bouwer

VANESSA BOUWER
Director: Information and Fund-Raising
S A NATIONAL COUNCIL FOR THE BLIND.

MESSAGE FROM THE WINNING PHOTOGRAPHER
Dawn of the New South Africa

I feel truly honoured to have produced the cover picture of this historic and wonderful book and hope the fruits of all our efforts will bless the people of this great new South African nation all of us are building. I must give thanks to Jesus Christ, in whom all things are possible, and all praise and glory to God the Father, who gave me the talent and vision to enjoy this life and partake in this worthy project.

I had such fun shooting pics for the first Day in the Life book twelve years ago (three of which were included) that, when I heard of the new project, I decided to give it my best shot. I studied the cover of the first book and then designed an image that would maintain continuity and express hope in our changing new South Africa.

Midnight 3 August arrived and I ventured out to see who lives in our new South Africa. As the night gave way to the promise of dawn, I woke my twelve-year-old son, Kyle, took our new South African flag and headed for the top of the koppie at the end of our driveway (near Nelspruit). Here, we chose a suitable vantage point, "flew" the flag to fit the image I had designed – and waited for the sunrise.

With a remote SB24 flash to light the flag, a graded filter to "help" the sunrise colour, F4S with 24mm lens, Provia 100 trannie, f11/4sec ... voila ... "Dawn of a Day in the Life of the New South Africa".

The rest of the day was filled with exciting, colourful, humorous, moving, interesting and proud images that made me glad to be a part of this project.

God bless us all ... Nkosi Sikelel' iAfrica ...

RICHARD WILSON
(Nelspruit)

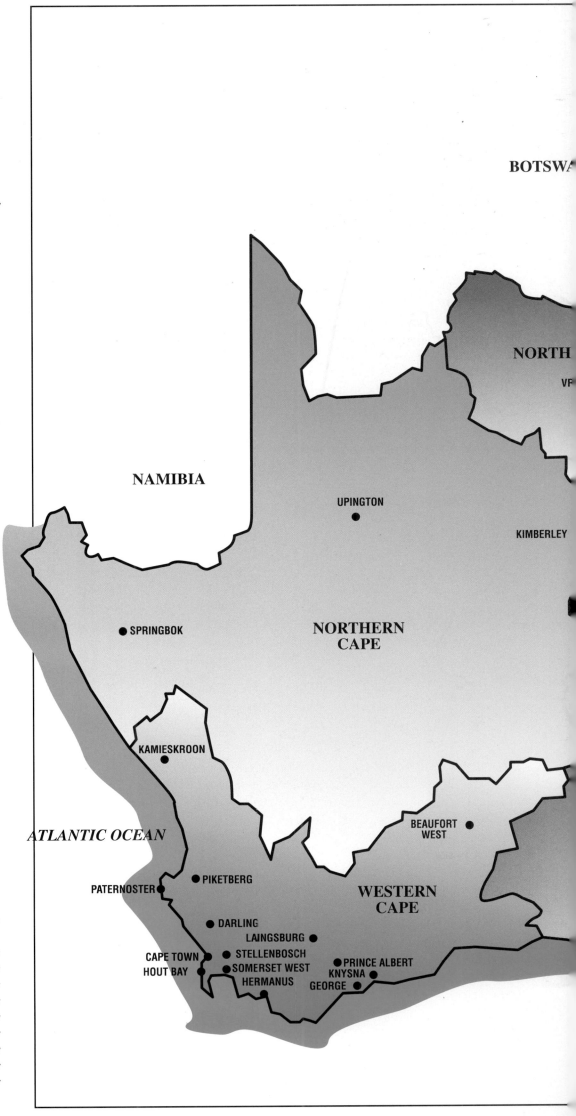

CONTRIBUTORS PAGE

The realisation of this book is the result of the personal contribution of thousands of professional and amateur photographers, the generosity of sponsors, the support of many trusting individuals who shared our enthusiasm, and the commitment of all the staff of the South African National Council for the Blind.

It would be impossible to acknowledge every entrant but we are immeasurably grateful to each and every one of you for, without your contribution, this book would never have materialised.

SUPPORTING SPONSORS

Old Mutual
The Conservation Corporation
Zulu Nyala Game Lodge
Mountain Shadows Manor House
Wilton Valley Game Reserve
Comair
Budget Rent-a-Car
The Blue Train
Vynide (Pty) Ltd
Photo-prints (Pty) Ltd
CTP
Standard Bank
Woolworths, Centurion Centre
A3I

THE PROJECT TEAM

Vanessa Bouwer
Colin Hall
Heather Nel
Di Pieterse
William Rowland
Bob Thornley
Janessa Urquhart

THE JUDGES

Bob Thornley (Chief Judge)
Vanessa Bouwer
Di Pieterse
Dawn Lindberg
Joe Myburgh
Peter Stuckey

MEDIA

The overwhelming support we obtained from the GMSA team, TV1, Sunday Times, and various daily and weekly newspapers assisted us tremendously in publicising our project. A very special thank you is due to the SABC Radio Active Unit for Public Service Announcements broadcast on all radio stations. These were supplemented by numerous radio interviews. We are eternally grateful to all print and electronic media for their assistance.